Adams

by Iain Gray

WRITING *to* REMEMBER

79 Main Street, Newtongrange,
Midlothian EH22 4NA
Tel: 0131 344 0414   Fax: 0845 075 6085
E-mail: info@lang-syne.co.uk
www.langsyneshop.co.uk

Design by Dorothy Meikle
Printed by Printwell Ltd
© Lang Syne Publishers Ltd 2022

All rights reserved. No part of this publication may be reproduced, stored or introduced into a retrieval system, or transmitted in any form or by any means (electronic, mechanical, photocopying, recording or otherwise) without the prior written permission of Lang Syne Publishers Ltd.

ISBN 978-1-85217-657-0

Adams

MOTTOES include:
Persevere and indulge not
(and)
In the cross is my salvation.

CRESTS include:
A demi-lion emerging from a ducal coronet
(and)
A gold cross crosslet.

NAME variations include:
Adam
Adamson
Addams
MacAdam
MacAdams
MacCaw

Chapter one:

Origins of Welsh surnames

by Iain Gray

If you don't know where you came from, you won't know where you're going **is a frequently quoted observation and one that has a particular resonance today when there has been a marked upsurge in interest in genealogy, with increasing numbers of people curious to trace their family roots.**

Main sources for genealogical research include census returns and official records of births, marriages and deaths – and the key to unlocking the detail they contain is obviously a family surname, one that has been 'inherited' and passed from generation to generation.

No matter our station in life, we all have a surname – but it was not until about the middle of the fourteenth century that the practice of being identified by a particular, or 'fixed', surname became commonly established throughout the British Isles.

Previous to this, it was normal for a person to be identified through the use of only a forename.

Wales, however, known in the Welsh language as *Cymru*, is uniquely different – with the use of what are known as patronymic names continuing well into the fifteenth century and, in remote rural areas, up until the early nineteenth century.

Patronymic names are ones where a son takes his father's forename, or Christian name, as his surname.

Examples of patronymic names throughout the British Isles include 'Johnson', indicating 'son of John', while specifically in Scotland 'son of' was denoted by the prefix Mc or Mac – with 'MacDonald', for example, meaning 'son of Donald.'

Early Welsh law, known as *Cyfraith Hywel*, *The Law of Hywel*, introduced by Hywel the Good, who ruled from Prestatyn to Pembroke between 915 AD and 950 AD, stipulated that a person's name should indicate their ancestry – the name in effect being a type of 'family tree.'

This required the prefixes *ap* or *ab* – derived from *mab*, meaning 'son of' being placed before the person's baptismal name.

In the case of females, the suffixes *verch* or *ferch*, sometimes shortened to *vch* or *vz* would be attached to their Christian name to indicate 'daughter of.'

In some cases, rather than being known for

example as *Llewellyn ap Thomas* – *Llewellyn son of Thomas* – Llewellyn's name would incorporate an 'ancestral tree' going back much earlier than his father.

One source gives the example of *Llewellyn ap Thomas ap Dafydd ap Evan ap Owen ap John* – meaning *Llewellyn son of Thomas son of Dafydd son of Evan son of Owen son of John*.

This leads to great confusion, to say the least, when trying to trace a person's ancestry back to a particular family – with many people having the forenames, for example, of Llewellyn, Thomas, Owen or John.

The first Act of Union between Wales and England that took place in 1536 during the reign of Henry VIII required that all Welsh names be registered in an Anglicised form – with *Hywel*, for example, becoming Howell, or Powell, and *Gruffydd* becoming Griffiths.

An early historical example of this concerns William ap John Thomas, standard bearer to Henry VIII, who became William Jones.

In many cases – as in Davies and Williams – an s was simply added to the original patronymic name, while in other cases the prefix *ap* or *ab* was contracted to *p* or *b* to prefix the name – as in *ab Evan* to form Bevan and *ap Richard* to form Pritchard.

Other original Welsh surnames – such as Morgan, originally *Morcant* – derive from ancient Celtic sources, while others stem from a person's physical characteristics – as in *Gwyn* or *Wynne* a nickname for someone with fair hair, *Gough* or *Gooch* denoting someone with red hair or a ruddy complexion, *Gethin* indicating swarthy or ugly and *Lloyd* someone with brown or grey hair.

With many popular surnames found today in Wales being based on popular Christian names such as John, this means that what is known as the 'stock' or 'pool' of names is comparatively small compared to that of common surnames found in England, Scotland and Ireland.

This explains why, in a typical Welsh village or town with many bearers of a particular name not necessarily being related, they were differentiated by being known, for example, as 'Jones the butcher', 'Jones the teacher' and 'Jones the grocer.'

Another common practice, dating from about the nineteenth century, was to differentiate among families of the same name by prefixing it with the mother's surname or hyphenating the name.

The history of the origins and development of Welsh surnames is inextricably bound up with the nation's frequently turbulent history and its rich culture.

Speaking a Celtic language known as Brythonic, which would gradually evolve into Welsh, the natives were subjected to Roman invasion in 48 AD, and in the following centuries to invasion by the Anglo-Saxons, Vikings and Normans.

Under England's ruthless and ambitious Edward I, the nation was fortified with castles between 1276 and 1295 to keep the 'rebellious' natives in check – but this did not prevent a series of bloody uprisings against English rule that included, most notably, Owain Glyndŵr's rebellion in 1400.

Politically united with England through the first Act of Union in 1536, becoming part of the Kingdom of Great Britain in 1707 and part of the United Kingdom in 1801, it was in 1999 that *Cynulliad Cenedlaethol Cymru*, the National Assembly for Wales, was officially opened by the Queen.

Welsh language and literature has flourished throughout the nation's long history.

In what is known as the Heroic Age, early Welsh poets include the late sixth century Taliesin and Aneirin, author of *Y Gododdin*.

Discovered in a thirteenth century manuscript but thought to date from anywhere between the seventh and eleventh centuries, it refers to the kingdom of Gododdin that took in south-east Scotland and

Northumberland and was part of what was once the Welsh territory known as *Hen Ogledd*, *The Old North*.

Commemorating Gododdin warriors who were killed in battle against the Angles of Bernicia and Deira at Catraith in about 600 AD, the manuscript – known as *Llyfr Aneirin*, *Book of Aneirin* – is now in the precious care of Cardiff City Library.

Other important early works by Welsh poets include the fourteenth century *Red Book of Hergest*, now held in the Bodleian Library, Oxford, and the *White Book of Rhydderch*, kept in the National Library of Wales, Aberystwyth.

William Morgan's translation of the Bible into Welsh in 1588 is hailed as having played an important role in the advancement of the Welsh language, while in 1885 Dan Isaac Davies founded the first Welsh language society.

It was in 1856 that Evan James and his son James James composed the rousing Welsh national anthem *Hen Wlad Fynhadad – Land of My Fathers*, while in the twentieth century the poet Dylan Thomas gained international fame and acclaim with poems such as *Under Milk Wood*.

The nation's proud cultural heritage is also celebrated through *Eisteddfod Genedlaethol Cymru*, the National Eisteddfod of Wales, the annual festival of music, literature and performance that is held across the nation and which traces its roots back to 1176 when Rhys ap Gruffyd, who ruled the territory of Deheubarth from 1155 to 1197, hosted a magnificent festival of poetry and song at his court in Cardigan.

The 2011 census for Wales unfortunately shows that the number of people able to speak the language has declined from 20.8% of the population of just under 3.1 million in 2001 to 19% – but overall the nation's proud culture, reflected in its surnames, still flourishes.

Many Welsh families proudly boast the heraldic device known as a Coat of Arms, as featured on our front cover.

The central motif of the Coat of Arms would originally have been what was borne on the shield of a warrior to distinguish himself from others on the battlefield.

Not featured on the Coat of Arms, but highlighted on page three, is the family motto and related crest – with the latter frequently different from the central motif.

Echoes of a far distant past can still be found in our surnames and they can be borne with pride in commemoration of our forebears.

Chapter two:

On the borderline

Derived from what for centuries has been the popular personal name Adam, and indicating 'son of Adam', Adams is a name that stretches back to the Biblical Book of Genesis to 'Adam', the 'first man', and the Hebrew word 'adama', meaning 'red earth'.

In Wales, Adams as a surname can be traced back to the twelfth century, but those who would come to bear the name have much earlier roots.

In common with many other Welsh people of today, flowing through their veins is a rich and heady brew of the blood of the ancient Britons and invaders in the form of Anglo-Saxons, Vikings and Normans.

Composed of the Jutes, from the area of the Jutland Peninsula in modern Denmark, the Saxons from Lower Saxony, in modern Germany and the Angles from the Angeln area of Germany, the Anglo-Saxons held sway in what became known as England and also in parts of Wales from approximately 550 to 1066.

They had usurped the power of the indigenous Britons – who referred to them as 'Saeson' or 'Saxones' – and it is from this that the Welsh term for 'English people' of 'Saeson', the Scottish-Gaelic 'Sasannach' and the Irish-Gaelic 'Sasanach' derive.

We learn from the *Anglo-Saxon Chronicle* how the religion of the early Anglo-Saxons was one that pre-dated the establishment of Christianity in the British Isles.

A form of Germanic paganism, with roots in Old Norse religion, it shared much in common with the Druidic 'nature-worshipping' religion of the indigenous Britons such as the Welsh.

It was in the closing years of the sixth century that Christianity began to take a hold in Britain, while by approximately 690 it had become the 'established' religion.

The first serious shock to Anglo-Saxon control came in 789 in the form of sinister black-sailed Viking ships that appeared over the horizon off the island monastery of Lindisfarne, in the northeast of England.

Lindisfarne was sacked in an orgy of violence and plunder, setting the scene for what would be many more terrifying raids on the coastline of not only England, but also of Wales, Ireland and Scotland.

An indication of the terror they brought can be found in one contemporary account of their depredations and desecrations.

It lamented how "the pagans desecrated the

sanctuaries of God, and poured out the blood of saints upon the altar, laid waste the house of our hope, trampled on the bodies of saints in the temple of God, like dung in the street."

Further invasion followed between approximately 950 AD and 1000 by the feared Northmen, and the coastline of Wales was repeatedly subjected to their raids – but, when not raping and pillaging, they established trading posts and settlements at modern day Haverfordwest, Fishguard and Caldey Island.

Through intermarriage, the bloodlines of the native Britons such as the Welsh became infused with those of the Anglo-Saxons and the Vikings.

But there would be another infusion of the blood of the 'Northmen' in the wake of the Norman Conquest of 1066 – a key event in the history of the British Isles that sounded the death knell of Anglo-Saxon supremacy and also Welsh independence.

By this date, England had become a nation with several powerful competitors to the throne.

In what were extremely complex family, political and military machinations, the monarch was Harold II, who had succeeded as king following the death of Edward the Confessor.

But his right to the kingship was contested by two powerful competitors – his brother-in-law King

Harold Hardrada of Norway, in alliance with Tostig, Harold II's brother, and Duke William II of Normandy.

On October 14, Harold II encountered a mighty invasion force led by Duke William that had landed at Hastings, in East Sussex.

He drew up a strong defensive position, at the top of Senlac Hill, building a shield wall to repel William's cavalry and infantry.

The Normans suffered heavy losses, but through a combination of the deadly skill of their archers and the ferocious determination of their cavalry they eventually won the day.

Morale had collapsed on the battlefield as word spread through the ranks that Harold, the last in a long line of Anglo-Saxon kings, had been killed.

William was declared King of England on December 25, and the complete subjugation of his Anglo-Saxon subjects followed, with those Normans who had fought on his behalf rewarded with lands – a pattern that would be repeated in Wales.

While the Adams name is not identified with any particular one of the nation's historic thirteen counties there is an early identification with the borderland between Wales and England known as the Welsh Marches.

Also known as the March of Wales and in

Welsh as *Y Murs* and in Latin as *Marchia Walliae*, large swathes of this borderland area were occupied at the point of a sword by Anglo-Normans, who became known as Marcher Lords.

In the thirteenth century, one of these ambitious and powerful lords was known to the Welsh as John ap Adam, who owned estates that included the parish of Tidenham, in the Forest of Dean in the modern-day English county Gloucestershire and which adjoined the border.

Installed by successive English monarchs on the border to 'contain and subdue' the frequently rebellious native Welsh, these lords were virtually a law unto themselves until their jurisdiction was abolished under the Laws in Wales Acts of 1535 and 1542 – that effectively annexed what had been the Principality of Wales to the English Crown.

What had been the Marcher Lordships were organised into what are now the Welsh counties of Breconshire, Carmarthenshire, Denbighshire, Glamorganshire, Monmouthshire, Montgomeryshire, Pembrokeshire and Radnorshire.

Under a succession of Welsh leaders who included Llywelyn ap Gruffudd, known as Llywelyn the Last, resistance to the English Crown had proved strong.

But it was brutally crushed in 1283 under

England's ruthless and ambitious Edward I, who ordered the building or repair of at least 17 castles and in 1302 proclaimed his son and heir, the future Edward II, as Prince of Wales, a title known in Welsh as *Tywysog Cymru*.

A heroic Welsh figure arose from 1400 to 1415 in the form of Owain Glyndŵr – the last native Welshman to be recognised by his supporters as *Tywysog Cymru*.

In what is known as The Welsh Revolt he achieved an early series of stunning victories against Henry IV and his successor Henry V – until mysteriously disappearing from the historical record after mounting an ambush in Brecon.

Some sources assert that he was either killed in the ambush or died a short time afterwards from wounds he received – but there is a persistent tradition that he survived and lived thereafter in anonymity, protected by loyal followers.

During the revolt, he had consistently refused offers of a Royal Pardon and – despite offers of rewards for his capture – he was never betrayed.

Chapter three:

Honours and distinction

Three bearers of the Adams name were prominent in early American revolutionary and political history.

Recognised as one of the Founding Fathers of the United States, Samuel Adams was the statesman born in 1722 in Boston.

One of the leading figures opposed to the British Parliament's taxation of the British-American colonies – which sparked off the colony's Revolutionary War with Britain – he was one of the representatives in 1774 to the Continental Congress in Philadelphia and helped to guide the congress towards issuing the famous Declaration of Independence in 1776.

Adams, who died in 1803, was a second cousin to John Adams, also recognised as a Founding Father of the United States, and who was the nation's second President.

Born in Boston in 1735, where he practiced as a lawyer, he became a prominent figure in the Revolutionary War, and served as President of the United States from 1797 to 1801 after serving for a time as Vice President under George Washington.

Adams, who died in 1826, was the father of

John Quincy Adams, born in 1767, and who served from 1825 to 1829 as the sixth President of the United States; he died in 1848.

Across the Atlantic from the United States to Ireland, Gerry Adams, known in Gaelic-Irish as Gearòid Mac Ádhaimh, is the Northern Irish Republican politician who was born in Belfast in 1948.

President of the nationalist party Sinn Féin and a leading figure in the Northern Ireland peace process, in 1983 he became the first Sinn Féin MP to be elected to the British House of Commons, for Belfast West – but, in line with his party's policy, he refused to take his seat in the House.

President of Sinn Féin since 1983, he was elected in 2011 as TD (member) of the Republic of Ireland Parliament, Dáil Éireann, representing the constituency of Louth.

He is also author of a number of books that include his 1982 *Falls Memories* and the 2007 *Irish Eye*.

Also in Irish politics, Ian Adamson, born in 1944, is the medical doctor and author who served from 1998 to 2003 as the Ulster Unionist Party member for Belfast East in the Northern Ireland Assembly.

A recipient of the OBE and a former Lord Mayor of Belfast, he is also a founder of the Ulster-

Scots Language Society and author of several books on religion, folk poetry and history, including his 1974 *The Cruthin*.

Also in politics, Allender Steele Adams, born in Glasgow in 1946 and better known as Allen Adams, was the Labour Party politician who served as a councillor on the former Strathclyde Regional Council from 1979 to 1983 and as MP for Paisley North from 1983 until his death in 1990.

Having served as Labour's Scottish Whip, he once famously described then Prime Minister Margaret Thatcher in the Commons as having "behaved towards Scotland with all the sensitivity of a sex-starved boa constrictor."

Following his death, his wife Irene Adams, born in 1947, took her husband's seat in the subsequent by-election.

She stood down as an MP in 2005 and was subsequently created Baroness Adams of Craigielea of Craigielea in Renfrewshire.

A leading promotor of ethical business, Richard Adams, born in 1946, is the British entrepreneur who in 1974 founded the UK Fairtrade organisation Tearcraft and, five years later, Traidcraft.

The inspiration for these organisations came through his Agrofax Labour Intensive Products

Company that imported crafts from farming communities in Bangladesh.

A founder in 1989 of the UK Fairtrade Foundation and a member of its board from 1992 to 1999, and the recipient of an OBE, he is the author of a number of books that include his 1991 *Shopping for a Better World* and, from 1993, *Good Business?*

With the popular Adams spelling variation of 'Adam', William Adam, born in 1689 near Kirkcaldy, Fife, was recognised as one of the foremost architects of his time and the father of three other famous architects.

The son of a stonemason, he was apprenticed to this craft at the age of 15, and by 1721 was in charge of architectural projects.

His major works in Scotland include Duff House, in Banff, built between 1735 and 1739, Chatelherault, the Lanarkshire seat of the Dukes of Hamilton, the House of Dun, in Angus, Haddo House in Aberdeenshire and Hopetoun House, near Edinburgh.

He died in 1748, and his three sons successfully emulated his architectural fame.

They were his eldest son, John, born in 1721 and who died in 1792, Robert (1728-1792) and James (1732-1794).

Robert and James, who were also accomplished interior and furniture designers, are recognised today as the developers of what is known as the 'Adam style.'

While John Adam designed a number of houses in Edinburgh, including Milton House in the Old Town, Robert and James, in addition to their magnificent work on private homes, are also recognised for public works that include Edinburgh City Chambers, Edinburgh's Register House, the former Assembly Rooms, Glasgow and the re-modelling of the Theatre Royal, in London's Drury Lane.

One particularly intrepid bearer of the Adams name was William Adams, the late sixteenth to early seventeenth century English seaman who was the inspiration for the character of John Blackthorne in James Clavell's best-selling 1975 novel *Shogūn*.

Born in 1564 in Gillingham, Kent, he was aged 12 when apprenticed to a shipyard owner and by the time he was aged 24 he had not only mastered shipbuilding but also astronomy and navigation.

Enlisting in the Royal Navy, he served for a time under Sir Francis Drake and saw action in 1588 against the Spanish Armada.

Leaving the navy to work as a navigator, or pilot, for the Barbary Company, in June of 1598 he set sail from Rotterdam as part of a fleet bound for the west coast of South America to trade a cargo of goods that included woollen cloth, mirrors, muskets and coats of mail.

But the fleet was scattered in severe storms and, while some ships made it back to Rotterdam, one of the vessels, the *Hoop*, was lost with all hands.

Adams had originally been aboard the *Hoop*, but fortunately for him he had transferred to the *Liefda* – and it was this vessel, having lost nearly 70 of its original crew compliment of 100 through sickness, that finally made landfall in April of 1600 at what is now Usuki in Japan's Ōita Prefecture.

Thrown into prison by Tokugawa Ieyasu – shortly before he was appointed to the powerful post of Shogūn – after Jesuit missionaries had claimed Adams and his fellow crewmen were pirates, they were eventually released after Ieyasu became impressed by Adams' knowledge of shipbuilding.

Ordered by the newly-appointed Shogūn to build what became Japan's first Western-style ship, the crew were rewarded by being allowed to leave Japan.

But the offer did not extend to Adams, because his skills were considered too valuable, and it was not until 1613 that he was finally granted permission to leave.

By this time, however, Adams had struck up a close friendship with the Shogūn and, having adapted to Japanese culture and customs, chose to remain.

Granted great honours and privileges and having acted as an adviser on diplomacy and trade with the West, he died in 1620 at Hirado, north of Nagasaki.

His grave marker remains to this day, while in 1934 the Japanese ambassador to Britain unveiled a monument to him in his hometown of Gillingham.

James Clavell's novel *Shogūn* was meanwhile adapted for the 1980 television mini-series of the name, starring Richard Chamberlain in the role of 'John Blackthorne', while *Shogūn: The Musical* opened on Broadway in 1990.

Chapter four:

On the world stage

Born in 1923 in Manhattan, New York, Donald James Yarmy was the actor, comedian and director better known by his stage name of Don Adams.

Lying about his age, he was aged 16 when he enlisted in the United States Marine Corps, serving in the Pacific Theater of Operations during the Second World War and taking part in the battle of Guadalcanal.

Hospitalised for more than a year after contracting the serious form of malaria known as blackwater fever, he later served for a time as a Marine drill instructor.

Pursuing a stage career at the end of the war, he became best known for his role of Maxwell Smart (Agent 86) in the television comedy series – some of which he wrote and directed – *Get Smart*.

The role netted him three consecutive Emmy Awards – in 1967, 1968 and 1969 – while he also provided voices from 1983 to 1985 for the animated series Inspector Gadget.

He died in 2005, while he was the father of the actress **Cecily Adams**.

Born in 1958, she died a year after her father,

and was best known for her role of Ishka in the *Star Trek: Deep Space Nine* television series in addition to penning lyrics for a number of commercial jingles and theme songs.

Born in 1946 in New York City, **Lynne Adams** is the American actress and playwright whose television credits include, from 1966 to 1971 and from 1973 to 1976, *The Guiding Light*.

The writer and producer of stage productions that include the romantic comedy *Two Faced* – on which the 2002 film *Make-Up* is based – she is the older sister of the actress **Brooke Adams**.

Born in 1949, her big screen credits include the 1979 *Cuba* and, from 2005, *The Legend of Lucy Keyes*.

Through her late father, Robert K. Adams, she and her sister are descendants of the former U.S. Presidents John Adams and his son John Quincy Adams.

The recipient of four Academy Award nominations for Best Supporting Actress – for the 2005 *Junebug*, the 2008 *Doubt*, the 2010 *The Fighter* and, from 2012, *The Master* – **Amy Lou Adams** is the actress born to American parents in Italy in 1974.

Also the recipient of five BAFTA nominations, her role in the 2003 *American Hustle* won her a Golden Globe Award for Best Actress in a Musical or Comedy.

Married from 1966 to 1980 to the hairstylist

Vidal Sassoon, **Beverley Adams** is the actress born to a Canadian mother and a U.S. Air Force father in Edmonton, Alberta, in 1945.

A former teenage beauty queen, her film roles include that of Lovey Kravezit in the *Matt Helm* series of films starring Dean Martin.

With big screen credits that include the 1954 *Creature from the Black Lagoon* and the 1965 Elvis Presley musical comedy *Tickle Me*, **Julie Adams** is the American actress born Betty May Adams in 1926 in Waterloo, Iowa.

Her autobiography, *The Lucky Southern Star: Reflections from the Black Lagoon*, was published in 2011.

On British shores, **Kelly Adams** is the actress born in London in 1979; her many television credits include *Hustle*, *Death in Paradise*, *Holby City* and *Bluestone 42*, while big screen credits include the 2009 *Bronson*.

In the early Adams heartland of Wales, **Tony Adams** is the actor born in 1940 in Anglesey.

Television credits include *General Hospital* and *Doctor Who*, while he is best known for his role from 1978 to 1987 of Adam Chance in the television soap *Crossroads*.

On radio and television, **Kaye Adams** was host

from 1999 to 2006 of the popular British daytime television talk show *Loose Women*; born in 1962 in Grangemouth, Stirlingshire, since 2010 she has been host of the BBC Radio Scotland daily phone-in programme, *Call Kaye*.

Bearers of the Adams name have also excelled in the highly competitive world of sport.

In the wresting ring, **Chris Adams** was the English judo competitor, professional wrestler, promoter and trainer also known by his nickname of "Gentleman" Chris Adams.

Born in 1955 in Rugby, Warwickshire, he was aged nine when he began judo training and went on to win both national and world championships.

Taking up professional wrestling when he was aged 23, he wrestled mainly in America in World Class Championship Wrestling and was the first to popularise the "superkick" finishing move.

Having trained the world champion wrestlers Scott Hall and Steve Austin, he died in 2001.

From wrestling to darts, **Martin Adams**, nicknamed "Wolfie", is the English professional player and three-time World Masters champion born in 1956 in Sutton, London.

It was after being made redundant by the bank with which he was employed that he turned professional in 1992 – captaining England from 1993/94 to 2013.

On the ice, **Vicki Adams** is the Scottish curler who, representing her nation was a member of the team that won the 2013 World Championship.

Born in Edinburgh in 1989 and, along with Eve Muirhead, winner of gold medals in 2008, 2009 and 2011 World Junior Curling Championships, she also won a bronze medal representing Great Britain at the 2014 Winter Olympics.

In the highly cerebral world of chess, **Michael Adams**, born in 1971 in Truro, Cornwall is the British Chess Grandmaster who, when aged 15, became the world's youngest International Master.

In the world of music, Victoria Caroline Adams is better known by her married name of **Victoria Beckham** and, as a member of the five-piece all-girl pop group Spice Girls as "Posh Spice".

Born in Harlow, Essex in 1974 and raised in Goffs Oak, Hertfordshire, the daughter of an electronics engineer and a hairdresser, she rose to fame with the Spice Girls in the late 1990s.

The band enjoyed a series of international hits that include the 1996 *Wannabe* and the 1998 *Viva Forever*, while since the band split she has pursued a solo career.

Married since 1999 to the former England international footballer David Beckham, she is also a highly successful businesswoman and fashion designer.

The recipient of a host of honours and awards, **Bryan Adams** is the Canadian rock musician and songwriter born in 1959 in Kingston, Ontario.

His albums include the 1980 self-titled *Bryan Adams*, and the 2008 *11*, while he also wrote and performed *(Everything I Do) I Do It for You*, featured in the 1991 film *Robin Hood: Prince of Thieves*.

Honours and awards include 15 Grammy nominations and the Order of Canada and the Order of British Columbia – not only for his contribution to popular music, but also for his philanthropic work through a foundation he set up to improve education for people throughout the world.

Inducted in 2006 to the Canadian Music Hall of Fame, he also has a star on the Hollywood Walk of Fame.

Behind the camera lens, **Eddie Adams** was the acclaimed American photographer and photojournalist who won a Pulitzer Prize for Spot News Photography and a World Press Photo Award for an iconic and harrowing image from the Vietnam War.

This was while, working for Associated Press,

he photographed Vietnamese police chief General Nguyen Ngoc Loan shooting a Vietcong prisoner dead on a Saigon Street in February of 1968.

Born in 1933, Adams also earlier served as a combat photographer with the United States Marine Corps during the 1950 to 1953 Korean War, while he is also noted for portraits of a number of celebrities and politicians.

The subject of the 2009 documentary feature *An Unlikely Weapon*, narrated by Keifer Sutherland, he died in 2004.

Born in San Francisco in 1902, Ansel Easton Adams, better known as **Ansel Adams**, was the pioneering American photographer famed for his black-and-white landscape images of the American West.

Overcoming illness and family poverty as a child and also a keen environmentalist, he went on to capture iconic images that include his 1941 *Moonrise, Hernandez, New Mexico*, *Mount McKinley* and *Old Faithful Geyser*.

Having developed, along with fellow photographer Fred Archer, the 'Zone System' in order to determine proper exposure and a co-founder of photography's Group f/64, he died in 1984.

Also behind the camera lens, **Robert Adams**, born in 1937 in Orange, New Jersey, is the contemporary

American photographer noted for his images of the changing landscape of the American West.

With books that include his 1974 *The New West* and the exhibition *New Topographics: Photographs of a Man-Altered Landscape*, his many awards and honours include having twice been awarded a Guggenheim Fellowship and also the Hasselblad Award.

In the world of the written word, best known as the author of *The Hitchhiker's Guide to the Galaxy*, **Douglas Adams** was the English writer and satirist born in 1952 in Cambridge.

The Hitchhiker's Guide to the Galaxy started as a BBC radio comedy in 1978, before Adams developed it into five books that remain international best-sellers; he died in 2001.

Born in 1920 in Wash Common, near Newbury, Berkshire, **Richard Adams** was the renowned author of *Watership Down*.

First published in 1972, it is now recognised as a classic, while before his death in 2016 Adams was the recipient of a number of awards that include the Carnegie Medal and a Guardian Award for Children's Fiction.

Starting to draw his own comics at the tender age of only six, **Scott Adams** is the American cartoonist and satirist best known for his internationally-syndicated *Dilbert* comic strip.

Born in Windham, New York in 1957 and a full-time cartoonist since 1995, his *Dilbert* strip takes a wry look at the lives of white-collar employees of large corporations.

No reference to bearers of the Adams name and its popular spelling variant of 'Addams' could perhaps be complete without at least a mention of the *Addams Family*.

The creation of the American cartoonist **Charles Addams**, the spookily eccentric family was featured in the *New Yorker* magazine from 1938 until his death in 1988.

It was through the 1960's American television comedy series *The Addams Family* that they came to international attention – featuring characters such as Fester, Gomez, Grandmama, Lurch, Morticia, Pubert, Pugsley, Thing and Wednesday.